Put Beginning Readers on the Right Track with
ALL ABOARD READING™

The All Aboard Reading series is especially designed for beginning readers. Written by noted authors and illustrated in full color, these are books that children really want to read—books to excite their imagination, expand their interests, make them laugh, and support their feelings. With fiction and nonfiction stories that are high interest and curriculum-related, All Aboard Reading books offer something for every young reader. And with four different reading levels, the All Aboard Reading series lets you choose which books are most appropriate for your children and their growing abilities.

Picture Readers

Picture Readers have super-simple texts, with many nouns appearing as rebus pictures. At the end of each book are 24 flash cards—on one side is a rebus picture; on the other side is the written-out word.

Station Stop 1

Station Stop 1 books are best for children who have just begun to read. Simple words and big type make these early reading experiences more comfortable. Picture clues help children to figure out the words on the page. Lots of repetition throughout the text helps children to predict the next word or phrase—an essential step in developing word recognition.

Station Stop 2

Station Stop 2 books are written specifically for children who are reading with help. Short sentences make it easier for early readers to understand what they are reading. Simple plots and simple dialogue help children with reading comprehension.

Station Stop 3

Station Stop 3 books are perfect for children who are reading alone. With longer text and harder words, these books appeal to children who have mastered basic reading skills. More complex stories captivate children who are ready for more challenging books.

In addition to All Aboard Reading books, look for All Aboard Math Readers™ (fiction stories that teach math concepts children are learning in school); All Aboard Science Readers™ (nonfiction books that explore the most fascinating science topics in age-appropriate language); All Aboard Poetry Readers™ (funny, rhyming poems for readers of all levels); and All Aboard Mystery Readers™ (puzzling tales where children piece together evidence with the characters).

All Aboard for happy reading!

To my great sand sculpture crew and especially Evan and Jennifer—C.S.

The illustrator (right) at a sand sculpture contest

GROSSET & DUNLAP
Published by the Penguin Group
Penguin Group (USA) Inc., 375 Hudson Street, New York, New York 10014, U.S.A.
Penguin Group (Canada), 90 Eglinton Avenue East, Suite 700, Toronto, Ontario, Canada M4P 2Y3
(a division of Pearson Penguin Canada Inc.)
Penguin Books Ltd, 80 Strand, London WC2R 0RL, England
Penguin Ireland, 25 St Stephen's Green, Dublin 2, Ireland
(a division of Penguin Books Ltd)
Penguin Group (Australia), 250 Camberwell Road, Camberwell, Victoria 3124, Australia
(a division of Pearson Australia Group Pty Ltd)
Penguin Books India Pvt Ltd, 11 Community Centre, Panchsheel Park, New Delhi - 110 017, India
Penguin Group (NZ), 67 Apollo Drive, Mairangi Bay, Auckland 1311, New Zealand
(a division of Pearson New Zealand Ltd)
Penguin Books (South Africa) (Pty) Ltd, 24 Sturdee Avenue, Rosebank, Johannesburg 2196, South Africa

Penguin Books Ltd, Registered Offices:
80 Strand, London WC2R 0RL, England

Text copyright © 2007 by Grosset & Dunlap. Illustrations copyright © 2007 by Carol Schwartz. All rights
reserved. Published by Grosset & Dunlap, a division of Penguin Young Readers Group, 345 Hudson
Street, New York, New York 10014. ALL ABOARD SCIENCE READER and GROSSET & DUNLAP are
trademarks of Penguin Group (USA) Inc. Printed in the U.S.A.

Library of Congress Control Number: 2006031177

ISBN 978-0-448-44567-0   10 9 8 7 6 5 4 3 2 1

Best Friends

The True Story of Owen and Mzee

By Roberta Edwards
Illustrated by Carol Schwartz

Grosset & Dunlap

This is a very old giant tortoise.

His name is Mzee.

(You say it like this: ma-ZEE.)

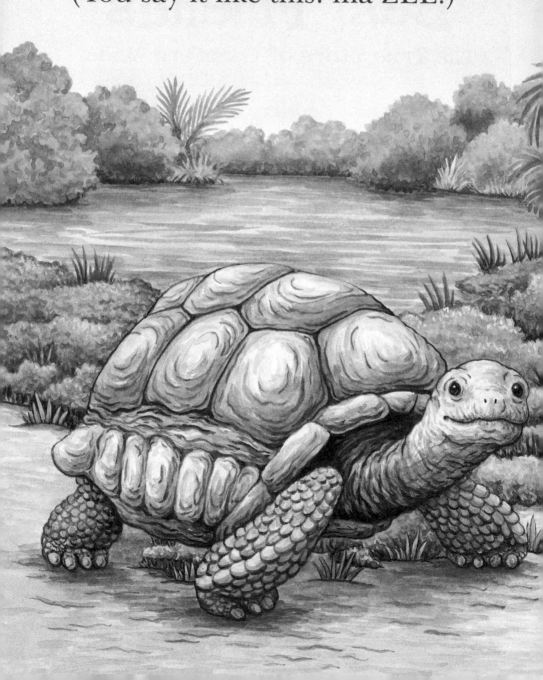

This is a baby hippo named Owen.

Mzee and Owen are best friends.

What do they have in common?

Not much.

Tortoises are reptiles.

So are crocodiles,
snakes, and lizards.

Hippos are mammals.

So are cows and dogs
and people, too!

Like all mammals,
mother hippos give birth
to live babies.
Owen was more than
50 pounds at birth.
He was about
three feet long.
That's a big baby!
Hippos are one
of the biggest
land animals on earth.
Only elephants and rhinos
are bigger.

Owen's mother took good care of him.
She fed him her milk.
She watched him play
with other little hippos.

He liked to roll in mud.

It kept him cool.

And it got rid of bugs.

Africa

Owen and his mother lived
with a group of hippos.
They lived near a river
on the east coast of Africa.
(The dark dot on the map
shows where.)
She and the older hippos
kept Owen and the other babies
safe from enemies.

Who are hippos' enemies?
Lions and hyenas
and crocodiles.

One day heavy rains came.
It rained and rained.

The river flooded.

The hippos were swept out to sea.

At last the storm ended.

Only one hippo was left.

Owen.

He was just one year old.

And he was all alone.

Still, he was lucky.

Some people saved Owen.

He was hard to catch.

But they got
the little hippo to land.
They named him Owen
after the man who caught him.

Owen needed a new home.
He could not care for himself.
But a new group of hippos
would just turn him away.

The best place was a special zoo.
Owen was driven there.
Haller Park became
Owen's new home.

Do you know who else
lived at Haller Park?
Mzee.
Mzee was the
oldest animal there.
He was 130 years old!
His name means
"wise old man."
Mzee lived by a pond.
He was not friends
with other animals.
Not the monkeys
or the bushbucks.
(Bushbucks look like small deer.)

But right away
Owen picked out Mzee.
He ran over to him.

Owen hid

behind the old tortoise.

Poor Owen!

He was scared.

Maybe Mzee looked like a hippo

to him.

Mzee hissed at Owen.

Mzee tried to get away.

But no matter where Mzee went,

Owen followed.

The next morning
Owen was curled up at
Mzee's side.
Mzee did not seem to mind.

Little by little

Owen and Mzee became friends.

Now they are best friends.

They take swims together.

They eat their food together.

They sleep side by side.

Owen has no mother.

He has Mzee.

Mzee has Owen.

That is enough for both of them.